Inspirations of the Heart

Book of Poetry

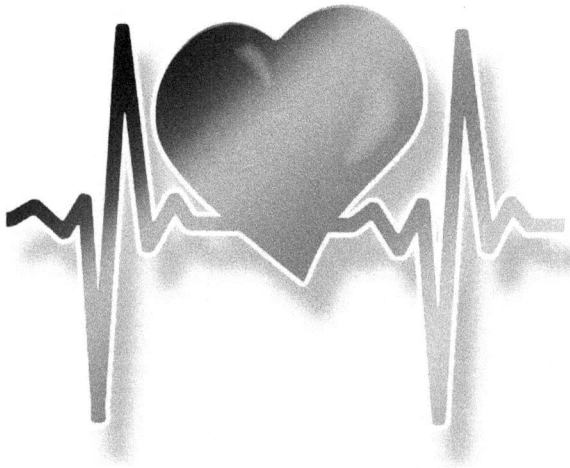

Inspirations of the Heart

Book of Poetry

Jacqui J. & ANTJ

Current Book By Jacqui J.

(Currently on Amazon)

The ABCs of Spiritual Living

*Inspirations of the Heart
through Scriptures*

SEAP
into becoming a better you

Declaring to SEAP
*Daily devotional
Guide to a better you*

RESET
*A time to relax, reflect, release,
and renew*

MINDSET
establishing an attitude that works for you

"49" Ways of Forgiveness

Foreword

Inspirations of the heart is a compilation of poetry and scriptures that inspires, motivates and encourages the soul. IOH- Book of Poetry speaks to twenty-two emotions that were brought to life from some of my favorite scriptures. These scriptures have been so encouraging to me in times of need, doubt, moments of sadness and just everyday emotions I've experienced. IOH-Book of Poetry seeks to inspire, encourage and reminds the reader of God's goodness.

Special Dedication

This book is dedicated to God, who is my ROCK, the center of my joy, my author and finisher of my faith, my peace, comfort, and Savior. Thank you God for blessing Amber and I with talents and gifts that can be shared to encourage and inspire your people. Shall these gifts and talents bring glory to you always and forever.

Acknowledgements

Acknowledgements begin with my loving family. My daughters, Latoria L. Johnson and Amber T.N. Johnson who inspires me to fulfill my passion and share my talents with others. Their support and inspiration moves me in the direction of being an example to them and others.

I want to acknowledge Amber T.N. Johnson, my youngest daughter for co-authoring this book and contributing her poems. Her poems touched me and are shared to demonstrate her talents. A special thank you for blessing the world with your God given talent. Thank you.

Inspirations
of the Heart
Book of Poetry

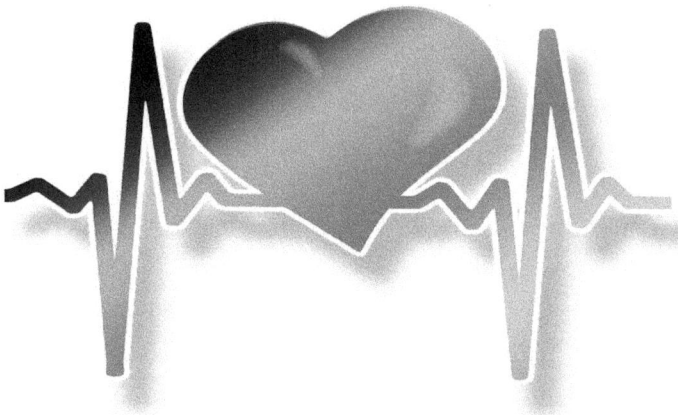

Table of Content

Joy

Loneliness

Love

Obedience

Strength

Trust

Trials

Triumphs

Wisdom

Acceptance

All are in need of acceptance.
Looking at life through vision of life's
pretense.
Running through life trying to fit in.
Wondering constantly when my
acceptance will begin.

Lord, I know your acceptance is all I
need.
Realizing that living a life trying to
please others will never help me to
succeed.
Finally understanding, when in fact the
acceptance really begins in me.
But somehow I find the acceptance hard
to see.

Reflecting on your word Lord has
helped the missing pieces to fit in.
Your word is a way for me to begin
again.

*Now understanding and knowing my
acceptance was embedded within.
God, you knew me, loved and accepted
me before it all began.*

1 Timothy 4:9
*This is a trustworthy saying that
deserves full acceptance.*

Admiration

In Admiration of You

Lord I sit in admiration of you.
There's nothing greater I'd rather do.
Respecting the one that gave me life.
Who gave his son for my sins and strife.
What an ultimate level of sacrifice.
Praising your name Jesus because you
paid that price.

Admiration of your beautiful wonders so
plentiful and true.
For this beauty you provide everyday
anew.
God, your unconditional love is unlike
any love I ever knew.
That's why it is so easy to be in
admiration of you.

You have made me wonderfully and fearfully.
This wonder in the image of you.
This I know all too well.
In admiration of you is where I dwell.
I'm just so grateful for all you do.
I'm just so blessed to be in admiration of you.

Psalms 139:14
I praise you because I am fearfully and wonderfully made; your works are wonderful, I know that full well.

Beauty

There's Beauty in who I am

*Does my character define the beauty
that's within?
Does it truly express where I have been?
People see what they want to see.
Shaping and molding me into who they
want me to be.
Looking internally beyond the exterior
is the key.
This often happens when one tries to
turn me into a we.*

*There's beauty in who I am.
Does my character say that I want to
live any other way.
Or does it say I'm settled or I'm on my
way.
Does my character say I don't deserve to
be loved by you today.*

Misunderstood sometimes and made to
feel alone because of the character
therein.
Simply by trying to hide the person
within.
All because of my need to fit in.
Are you looking at the internal
character inside?
Or are you trying to create a person that
will go along for the ride?

Listen, it is time you knew that this
person, this character, this beauty that
lies deep needs to be revealed.
My character and beauty only seek the
things that are real.
No time to play around and start
shaping me to fit the bill.

So, who am I?

I am a woman whose face of God I seek
No longer frail, weak or meek.

Someone that hears when he
call my name.
That someone who recognizes his voice
is one and the same.
Whose place is in that which is
proclaimed.
Designed to rest in a peaceful place.
All because of the beauty in his grace.

Who am I
Simply a child of GOD!

Psalms 27:4

One thing I ask from the Lord, this only
do I seek: that I may dwell in the house
of the Lord all the days of my life, to
gaze on the beauty of the Lord and to
seek him in his temple.

Blessings

*Blessings come in ways that sometimes
cannot be described
That moment when the unexpected
appears right before your eyes.
I know when I come to you God,
the hope for something good will appear.
Sometimes after fighting back a tear.
Then you, God you.
You know and knew but how could you?*

*That blessing comes just when I needed
it the most.
It was you but how can it be you.
How'd you know what I needed, but
you.
Oh, the beauty in you.
Brought forth through blessings in the
times when they are due.
Only you.
My blessings are found in you!*

Romans 15:29

I know that when I come to you, I will come in the full measure of the blessing of Christ.

Character

Character Within

Who understands the character within.
Who really knows where you have been.
All the struggles you still have within.
People say you have it altogether.
Who really knows the struggles and
storms you've had to weather.
When everything seemed to go wrong.
Holding on to that sweet calming
spiritual song.
You know the one that makes you feel
good and happy inside.
It seems to show up just when you want
to go and hide.
Is it pride that's clouding the view of my
character from the outside.
When really it is simply my stubborn
pride.
That pride I really need to leave behind.
Ripping through my character and

noticed from the outside.
Never understanding or being in touch
with the character on the inside.
The goodness that lies within minus the
pride.
Led by the spirit and created to live
right.
Everyone might not ever see what
remains out of sight.
Do away with all the pride within.
Allowing others to experience that
precious therein.
So, I'm saying – who really understands
this character within.
It's only the one who created it and
created it to WIN!

Romans 5:4-5
Perseverance, character, and character,
hope 5) And hope does not put us to
shame, because God's love has been
poured out into our hearts through the
Holy Spirit, who has been given to us.

Christianity

Being a Christian

Christianity doesn't mean that you are
perfect and free from flaws.
It's an opportunity to seek his name and
follow his laws.
Christianity doesn't mean you will
never sin.
It gives you an opportunity to seek
righteousness from within.
Christianity doesn't mean you will
never have pain.
It's a chance for you to seek the rainbow
after the rain.
Christianity doesn't mean you will not
have trials.
It's an opportunity to celebrate with
triumph and smiles.
Christianity doesn't mean you will not
have temptations.
It's an opportunity for you to pray and

seek revelations.
Christianity doesn't mean that you need
to shout to the rooftop.
It's an opportunity to praise HIM
diligently, never yielding or
willing to stop.
Christianity doesn't mean proving it
to man.
It's an opportunity to be an example
and serve HIM with all that you can.
Christianity doesn't mean seeking
acceptance from this earthly place.
It's an opportunity for you to seek HIS
will as you run life's race.

Being a CHRISTIAN is seeking God
above all, serving him, having a
relationship with him and simply
knowing that you are LOVED!

Romans 12:2

Do not conform to the pattern of this world, but be transformed by the renewing of your mind. Then you will be able to test and approve what God's will is – his good, pleasing and perfect will.

Christianity

Christ gave his life so you may
Have an opportunity to
Rest
In knowing your
Savior is always
There to keep you and
Inspire you with his love.
Always guiding your path and
Never leaving you
In times of need
Throughout your days.

Your Christianity is a dedication to
God!

Matthew 5:16

In the same way, let your light shine
before others, that they may see your
good deeds and glorify your Father in
heaven.

Devotion

His Will

Is it enough?
Enough to just say we are Christians.
When our faith is tested and our test
becomes our testimonies.
When we see other Christians falling
and we don't extend a hand to catch
them?
When we ask for prayer and we don't
commit to praying for ourselves?
When we are blessed daily and we don't
seek to bless others?
When we study God's word and don't
apply it to our lives.

Really is it ENOUGH?
Enough to praise God when things are
going well.
Praise HIM in the midst of our trials.

We must praise his name for all the accomplishments and for allowing us to see them.

Enough that we must recognize it was by faith and his mercy that brought us through the storm.

Let it be enough to praise him because he is your hope when it is gone.

Cease making excuses to devote time to him and don't waste it on judging others.

Come on is it ENOUGH?

Let's shine our light by being a light for others.

Give our testimonies so others will know they are not alone.

Catch them before and during their fall!

Pray without ceasing.

Live HIS WORD!

Find your purpose!

Praise him always!

Recognize his presence and call on HIM daily!

Is it ENOUGH?

You be the JUDGE!

Psalms 5:3

In the morning, Lord, you hear my voice; In the morning I lay my requests before You and wait expectantly.

Endurance

"Survive"

*When you feel that you have nothing
else to give
And the challenges of the world is more
than challenge you can bear to live
Hold on and find the strength God so
graciously gives from day to day.
Know things of today that bring forth
much sorrow.
Hoping it would not last and you will
soon find joy in your tomorrow.
Dig deep and endure while you find the
strength within
Know that Jesus is everlasting and
always your friend.
Lack of the endurance doesn't mean it
will not take some time.
That feeling of helplessness is certainly
not a crime.*

Just knowing all the things you cannot do.
Are truly the things with endurance can be shown through you.
Hold on and don' t give up because trouble won't last long.
Everything that seems impossible are the very things that make you strong.

Endurance is your state of surviving.
Allowing God to guide you while you are striving.
Endurance comes through your faith in Christ and the strength he has instilled in your life.

Colossians 1:11

Being strengthened with all power according to his glorious might so that you may have great endurance.

Endurance

How do you endure when the odds are
against you?
How do you endure when you don't
know what to do?
How do you endure when experiencing
financial challenges?
How do you endure when life does not
bring forth balance?
How do you endure when the pressures
of life are wearing you down?
How do you endure when in time of
need when there's no one to be found?
How do you endure through times of
sadness?
How do you endure through hard times
and madness?

Ready HOW do you ENDURE?

Pray, have patience and gain endurance
from God!

Romans 15;4

For everything that was written in the past was written to teach us, so that through the endurance taught in the Scriptures and the encouragement they provide we might have hope.

Arrived

*Arrived in a world where desiring to fit
in is a thing of life's norms.
Living life experiencing or own personal
quiet storms.
Always listening to what others have
to say.
When most of it will never help me to
find my way.
Living day after day living to
please others.
Keeping in mind that we should love
and care for one another.
When will I learn to please you?
Instead of pouring time into following
what others will do?*

*My journey and my path you
have paved.
Jesus died to pave my way.
Continuously falling off the course.
Instead of learning to rejoice.*

Rejoice in my FATHER's name.
It is why I still remain.

So be steadfast and hear me my dear.
You've finally arrived.
Just know I am near.
The picture and path is now very clear.
Face the challenge with no fear.
This mission I've set is well worth
the wait.
I just need you to live by FAITH!

You've ARRIVED!

Philippian 1:6

Being confident of this, that he who
began a good work in you will carry it
on to completion until the day of Christ
Jesus.

Faith

My faith is weak with no hope in sight.
The day is gloomy and it's dark
like night.
The world is changing not like before.
Things are out of control and normalcy
is no more.
People are ill with no cure in sight.
Fighting for their health with all
of their might.
There seems to be no hope for tomorrow.
Ridding the worries and casting away
the sorrow.
God, though we are living out the days
of Revelation.
Is this some kind of indication?
Indication of what's to be?
A ray of hope for our tomorrows?
A day that is not filled with such
sorrows?
Some sense of normalcy?
A new day of joy for all to see?

A day that is not dark as night?
A Faith that is strong and bright?

Thank you God that we can have faith
that gives hope for a tomorrow
and we can one day see the evidence of
what was once something to believe but
not seen.

Hebrews 11:1

Now faith is confidence in what we
hope for and assurance about what we
do not see.

Fear

Fear Within

There are times when fear is up
close and real.
The feeling inside yet to be revealed.
Will there ever be a day without
fear?
A day when each day is not filled
with a tear.
Tell me when will this fear go away?
I don't want to feel this way.
Somehow this feeling wants to stay.

You see this fear within has a
tendency to take over that
which is me.
I know you this is not how you
intended it to be.

You never gave me a spirit of fear.
So I say as I fight back this tear.
Grateful that your comfort and love
is greater than that I feel.
Just embracing your comfort and
love that is so real.

Gives me power, love and
self-discipline.

Thank you God!

2 Timothy 1:7

For the spirit God gave us does not
make us timid. But gives us power, love
and self-discipline.

Forgiveness

For I am grateful for the forgiveness
you give.
Seven times Seventy-seven you forgive
over and over again.
I know to forgive myself and others is
what I'm called to do.
Praise your name that your heart and
love forgives me too.
Forgiveness is not always easy to do.
It is a conscious choice found in you.

Forgive and you will be forgiven.
That is truly a sign of Christian living.

Luke 17:4

Even if they sin against you seven times
in a day and seven times come back to
your Saying "I repent

Guidance

Lost in the shadow of this world

I get lost in the happenings of this world.
Sometimes there are twists and twirls.
Seeking guidance and trying to find
what to do.
Should I wait or try to pursue it?
Pursue the answers for the trouble
revealed in this place.
Living each day like I'm running a race.
Teach me Lord, what I should do?
Live for the world or live for you.
Hands down I will choose the guidance
that comes from you,
Teach me your way and I shall live this
life to please you.

Guide me Lord with your guidance!

Psalms 25:5

Guide me in your truth and teach me,
for you are God my savior, an my hope
is in you all day long

Hope

There is hope in the plan I have for you.
Hope for tomorrow and all I can pursue.
Hope for happiness and love beyond all
I knew.
Hope for prosperity.
Hope for healing.
Hope for all eternity.
Hope for a brighter future.

I am so glad – I found hope in you.

Jeremiah 29:11

For I know the plans I have for you,"
declares the Lord, "plans to prosper you
and not to harm you, plans to give you
hope and a future.

Joy

The beauty I see on this day.
Joy in the breath I breathe.
The visions I'm allowed to see.
Joy in all there is to be.
Happiness I feel inside.
Joy I get from you that can't be denied.
Worry no more for the love I have
for you.
The joy I feel because of all that you do.
Things I can't explain.
The removal of all the pain.
I get joy, God when I think
about you.
How you love me, keep me, watch over
me, protect me and all things you've
promised you would do.
I get Joy, pure Joy when I think about
you.
I owe it all to you.

James 1:2-3

Consider it pure joy, my brothers and sisters, whenever you face trials of many kinds 3) because you know that the testing of your faith produces perseverance.

Loneliness

Alone, Empty, Sad
And
Lonely
All that is not of me.
Joy you will find and will come to be
removing all fear that is not found
in me.
Fear not for I am here.
I will never leave you.
Seek me and you shall
find all the happiness and rid the
loneliness inside.

Isaiah 41:10

So do not fear, for I am with you; do not
be dismayed, for I am your God. I will
strengthen you and help you; I will
uphold you with my righteous right
hand.

Love

So pure, so real.
The mere feeling that ignites within.
Uncontrollable at times
Held real tight and extremely hard to
find.
Love so precious and pure.
Sometimes certain and other times
unsure.
Often long for and never freely given.
It comes with a cost and something
unforgiven.
Love so unconditional and innately
driven.
It's all the things that come with a
part of living.

Love this word that holds power and
great meaning.
It's nothing negative yet negatively used.
To seek it is to understand it.

*To keep it is to see it, feel it and live it
and know it is to know God!
God's love is that which is all that is
given freely, unconditionally and purely
from YOU!*

1 Corinthians 13:4-5

*Love is patient, love is kind, It does not
envy, it does not boast, it is not proud. It
does not dishonor others, it is not
self-seeking, it is not easily angered, it
keeps no record of wrongs.*

Obedience

Proclaim

We are who we say we are!
But wait, do our actions show something
different?
Who are we fooling?
When the doors are closed?
When there is only you in sight?
When our tongues utter words that are
unkind?
When our priorities are not serving
you?
When we compromise our thinking and
actions?
When we are too tired to give you
praise?
Too tired to read your word?
Can't seem to speak a word about you?
Christians!

We are who we say we are when we chose to walk in obedience to you God. When we chose to align with your will for our lives.

Think about it, we are who we say we are.

Or are we?

Psalms 128:1

Blessed are all who fear the Lord, who walk in obedience to him.

Strength

The strength you will find

The strength you'll find is right there
inside.
It was there all along suppressed and
casted aside.
Believing in the impossible was so hard
to fathom.
Feeling so weak and daring to move
towards what's to come.
Stuck in a place of vulnerability.
Fearful of the strength and that
desired entity.
The need to dig deep terrifies you.
Don't worry my child, you see I have a
strength that is so real and so pure.

Trust in me, place your hand in mine.
Where you are weak, I am strong
forevermore.
The strength you will find, is the
strength inside.
Seeking me, strength you will find.

Philippians 4:13

I can do all this through him who gives
me strength.

Trust

I shall trust in you with all of me.
I shall believe in all I can't see.
I shall pray and follow your lead.
I shall seek your way and all that
will develop in me.
I shall have hope in you.
I shall accept the unconditional
love that is so pure and true.
Lord, I shall trust in YOU!

Proverbs 3:5-6

Trust in the Lord with all your heart
and lean not on your own
understanding; 6) in all your ways
submit to him, and he will make your
paths straight.

Trials

Nobody Said...
By ATNJ

Nobody said...
Life is gonna be easy so God gives you
the strength to get through it everyday.

Nobody said...
There wouldn't be tears and heartache,
so you just thank God no matter what

Nobody said...
You wouldn't feel things you feel inside,
that's why God gives you emotions to
deal with those feelings.

Nobody said...
Your dreams wouldn't come true that's
why God gives you strength to persevere.

Nobody said...
You couldn't be loved that's why God
gives you a family who loves you, so
cherish them always.

Nobody said...
You would be who you are but God
made you the way he wanted you to be.

Nobody's said...
You would have a destiny but God has a
purpose and a plan for your life.

Nobody said...
You would lose your way, that's why
God makes a path for you to travel but
you choose which road you go down.

Nobody said...
You would do some of the things you do
but God knew you would do those things
so he still gives you a choice.

Nobody said...
There would be rain and storms but God clears everything up and it's your choice to wither live in the rain or let God clear things up and let the sunshine in your life.

James 1:12

Blessed is the one who perseveres under trial because, having stood the test, that person will receive the crown of life that the Lord has promised to those who love him.

Triumphs

God kinda triumph

There is a great victory in knowing you.
Each day I feel that I achieve something
so precious and true.
This God kinda triumph is something
that cannot be explained.
The victories that come aren't the same.
This God kinda triumphs are blessings
after blessings.
Sometimes coming through many prayer
intercessions.
There is definitely victory in this God's
kinda triumph.
All it takes is a God kind of buy-in.

Psalms 118:7

The Lord is with me; he is my helper, I
look in triumph on my enemies.

Wisdom

Words that we speak
By ATNJ

Are words an expression for us to say
how we feel?
Or is the meaning behind each word
truly real?
We open up our mouths and don't seem
to truly care what comes out.
Half the time we don't understand what
the words we speak are about.
As we speak we should think before we
speak.
Our words should be moderate and
mild.
Much like the words of an innocent
child.
So take your words and search for a
deeper meaning.

Transform them into something that is not demeaning.
Words can kill!

The pain that we evoke in them is real. Watch what you say because words can turn someone's life a totally different way.

James 1:5

If any of you lacks wisdom, you should ask God, who gives generously to all without finding fault, and it will be given to you.

Inspirational Scriptures

Faith

Ephesians 2:8

For it is by grace you have been saved, through faith – and this is not from yourselves, it is the gift of God–

Hebrews 11:3

By faith we understand that the universe was formed at God's command, so that what is seen was not made out of what was visible.

Hebrews 11:6

And without faith it is impossible to please God, because anyone who comes to him must believe that he exists and that he rewards those who earnestly seek him.

Romans 8:28

And we know that in all things God works for the good of those who love him, who have been called according to his purpose.

James 1:3

Because you know that the testing of your faith produces perseverance.

Hebrews 12:2

Fixing our eyes on Jesus, the pioneer and perfecter of faith. For the joy set before him he endured the cross, scorning its shame, and sat down at the right hand of the throne of God.

James 2:17

In the same way, faith by itself, if is not accompanied by action, is dead.

Mark 11:22

"Have faith in God," Jesus answered.

Ephesians 3:17

So that Christ may dwell in your hearts through faith. And I pray that you, being rooted and established in love.

Romans 10:10

For it is with your heart that you believe and are justified, and it is with your mouth that you profess your faith and are saved.

HOPE

Jeremiah 29:11

For I know the plans I have for you," declares the Lord, "plans to prosper you and not to harm you, plans to give you hope and a future.

Hebrews 6:19

We have this hope as an anchor for the soul, firm and secure. It enters the inner sanctuary behind the curtain,

Matthew 12:21

In his name the nations will put their hope."

Romans 5:5

And hope does not put us to shame, because God's love has been poured out into our hearts through the Holy Spirit, who has been given to us.

Romans 15:13

May the God of hope fill you with all joy and peace as you trust in him, so that you may overflow with hope by the power of the Holy Spirit.

Romans 12:12

Be joyful in hope, patient in affliction, faithful in prayer.

Psalms 25:21

*May integrity and uprightness
protect me, because my hope, Lord,
is in you.*

Psalms 31:24

*Be strong and take heart, all you
who hope in the Lord.*

Psalms 62:5

*Yes, my soul, find rest in God; my
hope comes from him.*

Psalm 39:7

"But now, Lord, what do I look for?

My hope is in you.

LOVE

John 3:16

*For God so **loved** the world that he gave his one and only Son, that whoever believes in him shall not perish but have eternal life.*

Romans 5:8

*But God demonstrates his own **love** for us in this: While we were still sinners, Christ died for us.*

1 Corinthians 13:4

Love is patient, love is kind. It does not envy, it does not boast, it is not proud.

1 Corinthians 13:5

It does not dishonor others, it is not self-seeking, it is not easily angered, it keeps no record of wrongs.

1 Corinthians 13:6

Love does not delight in evil but rejoices with the truth.

1 Corinthians 13:7

It always protects, always trusts, always hopes, always perseveres.

1 Corinthians 16:14

Do everything in love.

1 John 4:7

Dear friends, let us love one another, for love comes from God. Everyone who loves has been born of God and knows God

Ephesians 4:2

Be completely humble and gentle; be patient, bearing with one another in love.

Exodus 20:6

But showing love to a thousand generations of those who love me and keep me commandments.

1 Corinthians 13:13

And now these three remain: faith, hope and love. But the greatest of these is love.

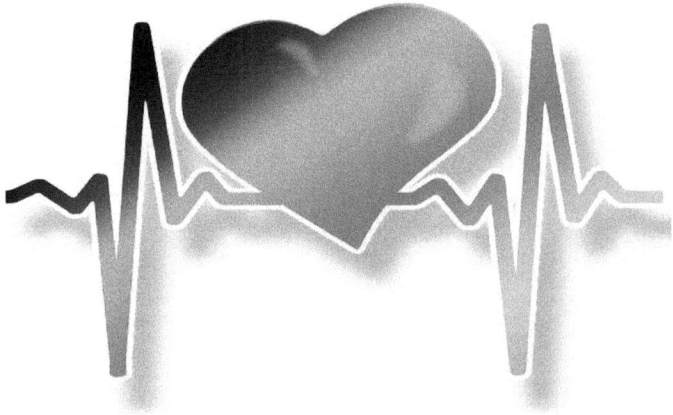

Reflective Moments

Here's an opportunity to reflect on what you have read and jot down your thoughts about what you have read or any feelings sparked from what you have read.

_____

_____

_____

_____

_____

_____

_____

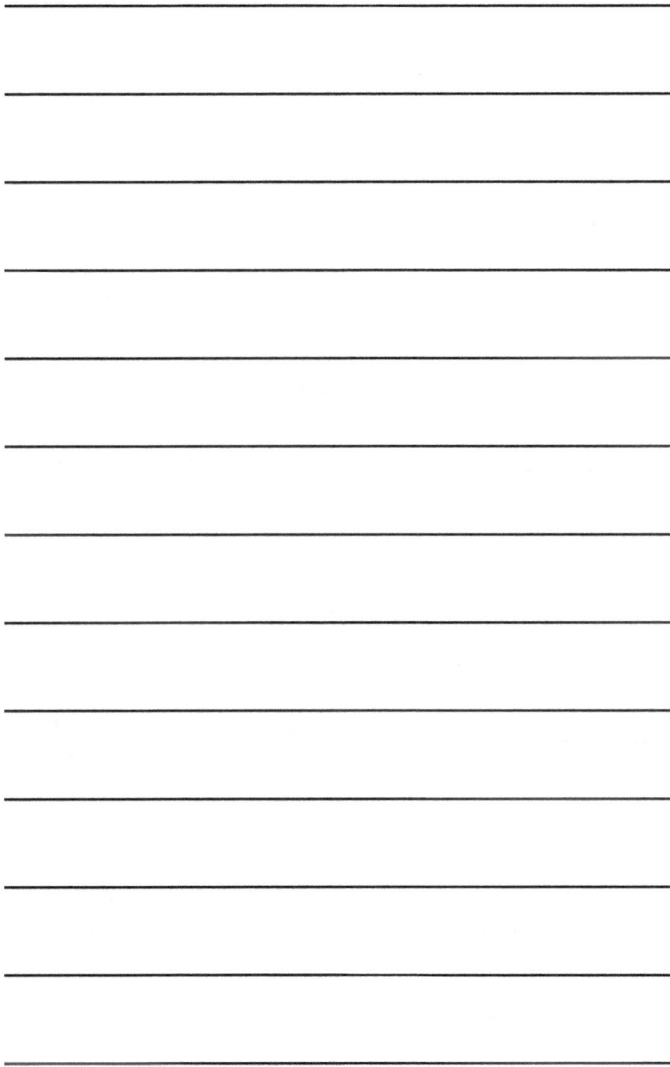

Authors' Message

To our readers, thank you for choosing to purchase and read this book. We don't take this lightly and appreciate your support. It is our goal to inspire and share God's word in all we do.

It is our prayer that this book inspired you and brought joy to your heart. This book was derived from the love and inspirations that God's word birthed in our hearts.

Be Blessed,

Jacqui J. & ANTJ

Inspirations of the Heart

Book of Poetry

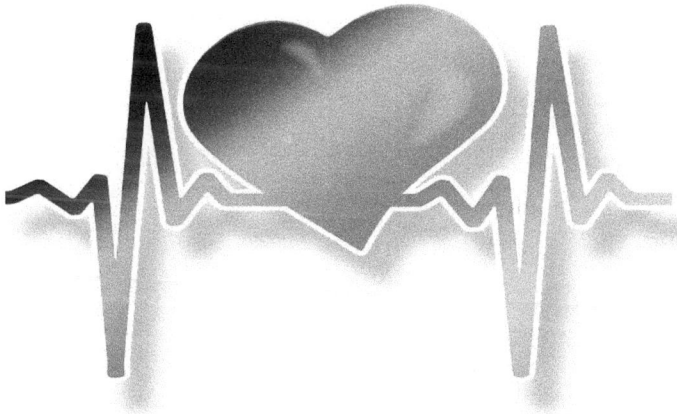

Jacqui J. & ATNJ

References

The Holy Bible, New International Version® NIV ® Copyright © 1973, 1978, 1984, 2011 by Biblica, Inc. ® Used by Permission of Biblica, Inc. ® All rights reserved worldwide.

www.ingramcontent.com/pod-product-compliance
Lightning Source LLC
Chambersburg PA
CBHW071237090426
42736CB00014B/3118

9 781735 552217